# THE LITTLE BOOK OF
# SASS

The Wit and Wisdom
of Jonathan Van Ness

# THE LITTLE BOOK OF
# SASS

## The Wit and Wisdom
## of Jonathan Van Ness

First published in Great Britain in 2019 by Trapeze
an imprint of The Orion Publishing Group Ltd
Carmelite House, 50 Victoria Embankment
London EC4Y 0DZ

An Hachette UK Company

3 5 7 9 10 8 6 4 2

A CIP catalogue record for this book is
available from the British Library.

ISBN Hardback 978 1 40919 162 9

Printed in Italy

MIX
Paper from
responsible sources
FSC® C023419

www.orionbooks.co.uk

# CONTENTS

# SASS

'MY DAD'S FRIEND ASKED WHAT I WANTED
TO BE WHEN I GREW UP AND I SAID I
WANTED TO BE EITHER A CABANA GIRL
OR A COSMETOLOGIST BECAUSE
THAT'S WHAT THIS GIRL WAS.'

**_VOGUE_**
14 June 2018

'BREAKER, ONE-NINE. THIS IS
JONATHAN VAN NESS COMING IN,
PULL THAT ASS OVER.'

**QUEER EYE**
Series One, Episode Three

'NEAL'S BATHROOM REMINDS ME A LOT OF A SKIN TAG. IT'S NOT HURTING ANYTHING, BUT IT DOESN'T LOOK GREAT.'

**QUEER EYE**
Series One, Episode Two

'WHEN YOUR BEST LOOK IS FRESH OUT OF BED SASQUATCH, IT IS NOT INSPIRING FOR YOUR LADY. AT ALL.'

**QUEER EYE**
Series Two, Episode Two

# 'STRUGGS TO FUNC.'

**QUEER EYE**
Series Two, Episode Five

'THERE IS A DIVA IN THERE, BUT ALL SHE NEEDS IS A LITTLE BIT OF A BOLD LIP.'

**QUEER EYE**
Series Two, Episode One

'IN MY WORLD, EVERYTHING THAT'S
ROMANTIC IS TOPLESS.'

**QUEER EYE**
Series Two, Episode Two

# 'THIS IS LIKE
# BOYFRIEND-MATERIAL HOUSE!'

**QUEER EYE**
Series Two, Episode Four

## 'I LOVE STRAIGHT PEOPLE.'

### *QUEER EYE*
Series One, Episode Eight

'DUE TO THE FACT THAT I WAS A MALE CHEERLEADER, IT'S VERY HARD TO EMBARRASS ME.'

**VMAN**
19 April 2018

'IT WASN'T AN OPTION FOR ME TO BE
CLOSETED OR TO KEEP IT TO MYSELF.
SKY'S BLUE, GRASS IS GREEN.
CAN'T FIGHT IT.'

**QUEER EYE**
Series One, Episode Four

'SHAMAZING.'

**QUEER EYE**
Series One, Episode Five

'I THINK HOW MUCH I'D TELL MY BEST
FRIEND: "QUEEN, LEAVE HIM, HE'S NO
GOOD," AND THINK MAYBE I NEED
TO TELL MYSELF THAT MORE.'

**ATTITUDE**
21 June 2018

'I LIKE TO PLAY. I LIKE TO EXPLORE. I DON'T
LIKE TO BE PUT INTO BOXES.'

**LA TIMES**
16 November 2018

'CAN YOU BELIEVE?'

**QUEER EYE**
Series One, Episode One

# 'YOU'VE JUST GOT TO TRUST WHAT THE GAYS TELL YOU TO DO.'

**QUEER EYE**
Series One, Episode One

'LIKE HE'S JUST GIVING YOU
BASIC, BASIC, BASIC.'

**QUEER EYE**
Series One, Episode Seven

'YOU'RE GIVING ME STRONG MAN, "I WILL CHANGE YOUR TYRE, I WILL PAY YOUR BILLS, I WILL PROVIDE."'

**QUEER EYE**
Series One, Episode Seven

'I JUST LOVE AN AIRPLANE TREAT. I FEEL LIKE MACAULAY CULKIN IN *HOME ALONE*, BUT IN FIRST CLASS.'

**ELLE**
20 June 2018

'I LOVE TO EXERCISE, I LOVE TO SKATE BUT I ESPECIALLY LOVE TO EXERCISE MY FIRST AMENDMENT RIGHTS.'

**JIMMY KIMMEL LIVE**
21 December 2018

'I LOVE ANYTHING WITH BUBBLES, SO I LOVE A FROSÉ MOMENT—I LIVE FOR A FROSÉ SLUSHIE.'

**WELL AND GOOD**
31 May 2018

'YOUR BODY IS FIERCE, IT'S CUTE,
IT'S FINE.'

**_ALLURE_**
23 March 2018

'BEST TRAVEL EXPERIENCE IS ANYTHING THAT INVOLVES TURQUOISE WATER.'

**REFINERY29**
20 December 2018

'I WANNA BE A NEW YORK–BASED
BABY FOR A WHILE.'

***HERE* MAGAZINE**

'WHAT AM I DOING ALL OF THIS WORK
FOR IF I'M NOT GOING TO SHOW
OFF A BIT?'

**JIMMY KIMMEL LIVE**
21 December 2018

'I'M JONATHAN AND I DON'T DO UNISON LINES.'

**MARIE CLAIRE**
12 July 2018

'NOTHING IS SCARIER THAN WHEN YOU LOOK DOWN AT YOUR CELL PHONE AND SHE'S AT 1%.'

**GOOD MORNING AMERICA**
5 November 2018

# POSITIVITY AND CONFIDENCE

'MY BEAUTY IS IN MY HEART.'

**HARPER'S BAZAAR**
20 April 2018

'IF YOU'RE FEELING A
NEVER FULLY DRESSED
HEEL. BUT ONLY IF
YOU NEED

LITTLE DOWN, YOU'RE
WITHOUT A STRONG
YOU'RE DEPRESSED — IF
A PICK-ME-UP.'

**PAGE SIX**
25 June 2018

'YOU WANNA HAVE YOURSELF LOOKING
TOGETHER, AS MUCH AS YOU CAN.'

**QUEER EYE**
Series One, Episode Six

'I HEAR MYSELF.'

**HARPER'S BAZAAR**

20 April 2018

'I NEVER WANT PEOPLE TO FEEL LIKE THEY AREN'T GAY ENOUGH OR STRAIGHT ENOUGH IT'S ABOUT WHAT'S IN YOUR HEART. AND WHAT'S IN YOUR HEART IS LIKE [KISSING SOUNDS].'

**QUEER EYE**
Series One, Episode Four

'LETTING PEOPLE IN ISN'T A SIGN OF WEAKNESS, IT'S A SIGN OF STRENGTH.'

### *QUEER EYE*

Series One, Episode Two

'I'M A BIG PROPONENT

WINNING AND LOVE

OF ALL LOVE

JUST BEING **FAB.**'

**THE DAILY MEAL**
22 July 2018

'CAN YOU HANDLE THE CON-FI-DONCE?'

**QUEER EYE**
Series Two, Episode Six

'I DON'T ALWAYS WANNA BE ALONE,
BUT I DEFINITELY LIKE POCKETS OF
SOLITUDE TO RECHARGE AND COME
BACK TO MYSELF. I THINK THAT'S
SO IMPORTANT FOR EVERYONE.'

**INSTYLE**
16 April 2018

'I FEEL IT'S BEEN SO FUN LIVING MY ADULT LIFE. I GET TO BE MYSELF.'

**THE CUT**
24 July 2018

'YOU'RE STRONG, YOU'RE A
KELLY CLARKSON SONG,
YOU GOT THIS.'

**QUEER EYE**
Series Two, Episode Six

'WE'RE JUST LITTLE BABIES DOING
THE BEST WE CAN WITH WHAT
WE KNOW, HONEY.'

**VULTURE**
21 February 2018

'I THINK THAT IT'S ALSO JUST LIKE PRACTISING CONFIDENCE, YOU KNOW, AND BEING ABLE TO FAKE IT UNTIL YOU MAKE IT AND THEN AT SOME POINT YOU DO BELIEVE IT, BECAUSE I DO LOVE MYSELF BUT I THINK THAT THERE'S DAYS THAT ARE EASIER THAN OTHERS TO SAY THAT.'

**BUSTLE**
28 February 2018

'IT'S OKAY. DON'T CRY! UNLESS YOU'VE
REALLY GOT TO CRY IT OUT, THEN I'M
HERE FOR YOU FOR THAT.'

**_RACKED_**
29 June 2018

'FOR ME, IT'S WAY MORE ABOUT THE
INSIDE THAN THE OUTSIDE.'

**DAZED**
19 April 2018

'DID I KNOW THIS WAS MY

DID I TAKE IT?

MOMENT TO SHINE? 100%.

# TAKE A LOOK!'

**QUEER EYE**
Series One, Episode Eight

'DON'T LET SOMEONE THINK YOU'RE NOT CUTE ENOUGH BECAUSE YOU DON'T KNOW HOW TO DO SOMETHING.'

**THE CUT**
24 July 2018

'I KIND OF WANT PEOPLE TO GET TO
WHERE THEY WANT TO GET, I JUST
WANT TO HELP THEM GET THERE
IN THE HEALTHIEST, BEST
WAY POSSIBLE.'

**BUSTLE**
28 February 2018

'IT'S ABOUT GOING TO PLACES THAT
ARE MAYBE NOT SO ACCEPTING AND
TRYING TO FIND THE GROUNDS THAT
YOU CAN CONNECT ON AS OPPOSED
TO FIGHTING OR REALLY LIVING
IN YOUR SEPARATION.'

**HERE MAGAZINE**

'NAMASTE, WE'VE ALL MADE MISTAKES, YOU KNOW WHAT I MEAN? WE'RE ALL DESERVING OF FORGIVENESS.'

**BUSY TONIGHT**
22 January 2019

# SELF-CARE

'I THINK ALL OF US FEEL PRESSURE.
THAT'S SO MUCH OF WHAT LIFE IS,
GETTING THROUGH IT IN A BALANCED
WAY WHERE YOU CAN STILL LOOK AT
YOURSELF IN THE MIRROR AND BE LIKE,
"GOOD JOB, GIRL. I LOVE YOU."'

**VULTURE**
21 February 2018

'I WANT TO SHOW STRAIGHT MEN AND GAY MEN ALIKE THAT SELF-CARE AND GROOMING ISN'T MUTUALLY EXCLUSIVE WITH LIKE, FEMININITY OR MASCULINITY.'

### QUEER EYE

Series One, Episode Six

♡

'HOW YOU TAKE CARE OF YOURSELF
IS HOW THE WORLD SEES YOU.
IT'S OKAY TO HAVE A RELATIONSHIP
WITH YOURSELF.'

**QUEER EYE**
Series One, Episode One

'WE FOCUS SO MUCH ON
OTHER PEOPLE AND BEAUTY
YOUR RELATIONSHIP

OUR RELATIONSHIPS WITH

FOR ME IS ABOUT FACILITATING

# WITH YOURSELF.

**VOGUE**
14 June 2018

'IN SERVICE INDUSTRIES, WE CAN BE SO PEOPLE-PLEASER-Y THAT YOU DON'T KNOW HOW TO SET YOUR OWN BOUNDARIES. AS I GET OLDER, THE MORE I'M LIKE, "NO—YOU HAVE TO SET A BOUNDARY."'

**VANITY FAIR**
17 April 2018

♡

'YOU HAVE TO CREATE LITTLE POCKETS OF JOY IN YOUR LIFE TO TAKE CARE OF YOURSELF.'

**QUEER EYE**

Series One, Episode Eight

'I'LL JUST STAY PUT, CATCH UP AND BINGE,
AND GET TO KNOW MY COUCH ON
A DEEPER LEVEL.'

**VMAN**
19 April 2018

♡

'THE BIGGEST THING ABOUT SELF-CARE
IS TO BE GENTLE WITH YOURSELF AND
REMEMBER THERE'S NO ONE WAY
UP THAT MOUNTAIN.'

**_TIME OUT_**
10 July 2018

♡

'SELF-CARE IS THE
THE THING THAT

NON-NEGOTIABLE. THAT'S

YOU **HAVE** TO DO.'

*DAZED*
19 April 2018

'IF I DON'T WORK OUT IN THE MORNING, I WILL HARM THE SHIT OUT OF EVERYBODY — MYSELF, YOU AND THE PEOPLE TRYING TO TALK TO ME, HONEY.'

**TIME OUT**
10 July 2018

♡

'I LIVE OFF COFFEE UNTIL 3 IN THE
AFTERNOON, AND THEN I TRY TO
BE BALANCED, BUT THE NEXT THING
I KNOW I'M FACE DOWN IN A
PLATE OF GARLIC BREAD.'

**ELLE**
20 June 2018

♡

# BEAUTY

# 'POMADE! POMADE! POMADE!'

## *QUEER EYE*
Series Two, Episode Eight

'SPRAY, DELAY,

# WALK AWAY.'

**QUEER EYE**
Series Two, Episode Two

'YOU WANT TO BE MORE HAIRY, THAT'S BEAUTIFUL. YOU WANT TO BE MORE CLEAN-SHAVEN, THAT'S GREAT.'

**_FASHIONISTA_**
7 February 2018

'A GOOD TIP FOR EVERYONE TO REMEMBER IS TAKE THAT MASK DOWN TO YOUR DÉCOLLETÉ, DON'T FORGET ABOUT HER.'

**VOGUE**
14 June 2018

'GETTING TO DO HAIR IS ALMOST LIKE
DOING STAND-UP WHILE MAKING
PEOPLE LOOK BETTER.'

**PEOPLE**
6 September 2018

'SO OFTEN GROOMING IS MEANT TO MAKE YOU FEEL BETTER ABOUT YOURSELF, AND A LOT OF TIMES WE USE IT TO MAKE OURSELVES FEEL WORSE. I REALLY WANTED TO USE THIS OPPORTUNITY TO MAKE THEM FEEL BETTER ABOUT THEMSELVES, NOT WORSE.'

**FASHIONISTA**
7 February 2018

'I WOULD SAY A KEY TO LIKING

# WHAT MOTHER

YOUR HAIR IS EMBRACING

NATURE GAVE YOU,'

**INSTYLE**
16 April 2018

'CHANGE YOUR PILLOWCASES
EVERY WEEK.'

**METRO**
21 December 2018

I FEEL LIKE IF YOU'RE SPENDING THE NIGHT GIVING YOURSELF A BLOWOUT, AND YOU DON'T FEEL COMFORTABLE WITH THE BLOWOUT OR YOU'RE HATING IT, IT'S GONNA RUIN YOUR NIGHT. IT'S ABOUT LISTENING TO WHAT YOU WANT AND WHAT YOU NEED, AND YOUR GLAM.'

**WELL AND GOOD**
31 May 2018

'I WEAR MY HAIR UP FOR PRIDE TYPICALLY, BECAUSE I CANNOT EVEN.'

**ELITE DAILY**
22 June 2018

'MAKE SURE YOU HAVE YOUR FLOSS
WITH YOU, HONEY.'

**REFINERY29**
20 December 2018

'IF THE FIRST INGREDIENT IS ALCOHOL, OR SOME TYPE OF WORD YOU CAN'T PRONOUNCE, IT'S NOT LOOKING GOOD.'

**_COSMOPOLITAN_**
18 June 2018